Everything
You Need to
Know About

Healing from Rape Trauma

The devastating crime of rape can damage a person's belief that she is in charge of her own life.

Everything You Need to Know About Healing from Rape Trauma

Cheryl Branch Coppin, FNP

The Rosen Publishing Group, Inc.
New York

Published in 2000 by The Rosen Publishing Group, Inc.
29 East 21st Street, New York, NY 10010

Library of Congress Cataloging-in-Publication Data

Coppin, Cheryl Branch.
　　Everything you need to know about healing from rape trauma / Cheryl
　　Branch Coppin.
　　　　p. cm. — (The need to know library)
　　Includes bibliographical references and index.
　　Summary: Identifies the nature, causes, and victims of rape, discusses
common misconceptions about it, and offers advice on healing from sexual
assault.
　　ISBN 0-8239-3122-6
　　1. Rape—Juvenile literature. 2. Rape victims—Juvenile literature. 3. Rape
trauma syndrome—Juvenile literature. [1. Rape.] I. Title. II. Series.

HV6558.C66 2000
362.883—dc21

99-049583

Manufactured in the United States of America

Contents

Introduction

Nina Kim's parents were in the middle of a divorce. When Mr. Kim brought Nina and her sister back from his weekend visitation, Mrs. Kim let him into the house. He said that he wanted to talk to her about getting back together. But after Nina and her sister went to bed, Mr. Kim pulled out a knife and forced Mrs. Kim to have sex.

Some guys who graduated last year came back to town and wanted to go out. A crowd of us went to one guy's house. I remember sitting at the counter watching him mix drinks. Then the next thing I knew, it was dark and he was on top of me.

He said I owed him because he took me to a movie. After he was done forcing me to have sex, he asked if I wanted to go out again the next night.

Shari, a high-school junior, had planned to go with her parents and her two brothers on a weekend camping trip, but at the last minute she decided to stay home to study for finals. On Saturday night, a burglar broke in. First he took the television and stereo, then he raped Shari.

Many people share a false belief about rape: They think that it is about sex. Some even go a step further and think that if a woman gets raped, it is because she "asked for it"—that is, she was raped because she did something to sexually arouse the rapist.

These ideas are wrong. Rape, sometimes described as sexual assault, is not about sex. It also is not about physical attraction. Rape is about power and violence. It is one person thinking that he or she has the right to use another person's body, no matter what the other person wants. No one asks to be raped, and no one is responsible for another person's behavior. No matter what the circumstances, rape is never the victim's fault. The rapist is always responsible for his own actions.

Rape can happen to any person, of any age, anywhere, at any time. Often it is a matter of bad luck—being in the wrong place at the wrong time. Rape can be especially damaging to the victim when the rapist is someone that she knows. In such cases, the victim is especially likely to feel that she did something wrong, that she is somehow responsible for being raped, or that there is something wrong with her ability to judge other people and decide who is a trustworthy friend.

All violent crimes damage the victim's belief that he or she is in charge of his or her own life and that he or she can make good decisions about how to behave and how to choose friends. But more than any other violent crime, rape violates a person's most private sense of self.

Emotional and physical recovery from rape can take a long time. The victim will need to talk about the experience, but often family and friends don't know what to say or how to act. Sometimes the police are involved and there is a trial. This book discusses how the law works for the victim and what support services are available. It also offers advice on what to do if you or someone you know is the victim of rape.

A Note About the Language in This Book

In this book, the words "victim" and "survivor" are used to describe anyone who is sexually assaulted or raped. The word "assailant" is used as a term for someone who commits any kind of sexual assault, including rape.

This book usually refers to victims and survivors of rape as "she" and assailants as "he" because statistically, females are far more likely to be victims and survivors and males are more likely to be assailants.

But the information in this book is vital for young men, too. Males can be raped or coerced (forced) into having unwanted sex just as females can. In addition, young men may be the brothers, boyfriends, or friends of someone who is a victim of sexual assault. As such, their support is just as valuable as support from females in helping a victim overcome her traumatic experience.

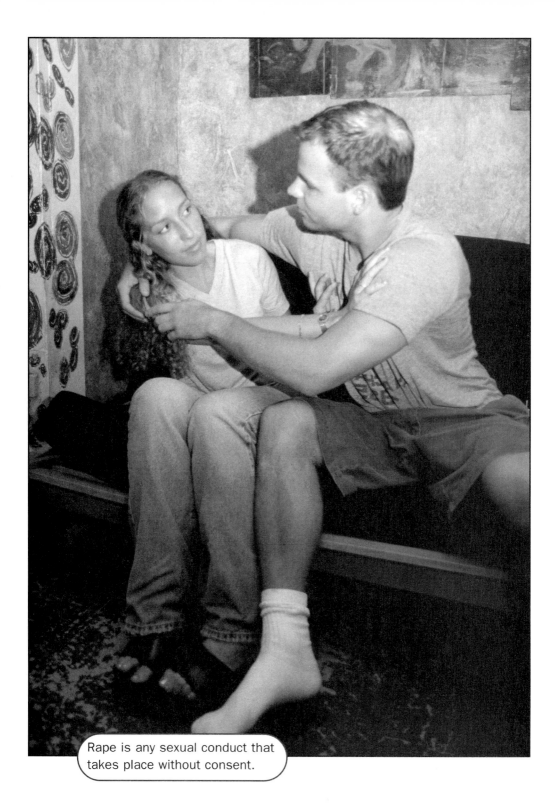

Chapter One

What Is Rape?

My friend Randy called me with a surprise. She just said to get dressed to go out for the evening. When she and her boyfriend and another couple came by, I saw what the surprise was: They'd brought Jason, a guy I'd gone out with a few times last year before he moved away.

All six of us went to a movie and hung out at the mall for a while and then went over to Randy's boyfriend's house. I sat at the counter and watched Jason mix us drinks. I thought it was just fruit juice and soda water.

The next few hours aren't very clear in my mind. I remember being in the living room with the lights off and nobody else being around besides Jason. He was having sex with me and all my clothes were gone. Then Randy was there, all

*upset, saying that she was taking me to the hos-
pital, that Jason had raped me. Later she told me
that she'd heard that he had done something like
this before but that she hadn't believed it.*

In most states, rape is legally defined as any form of
sexual conduct (behavior) carried out upon a person
against that person's will. Rape can occur under many
different circumstances, including the following:

- The assailant uses force or the threat of force to
  overpower or control the victim. Holding somebody down and having sex with him or her
  when the person has said no is rape.

- The victim is too young to give legal consent
  (agreement) for sex. This is the basis for what
  are called statutory rape laws. Even if the victim says yes, the law says that having sex with
  him or her is rape. The legal age of consent
  differs from state to state. To find out what it
  is in your state, contact your local district
  attorney's office. (You can find the telephone
  number by looking in the blue pages or
  Government section of the phone book under
  District Attorney.)

- The victim is not able to rationally decide
  whether he or she is willing to have sex because
  he or she is intoxicated or has a mental disorder.

> If a guy has sex with a girl who has passed out
> from drinking too much, it is rape.

In the scenario at the beginning of this chapter, the victim would fall into the last category listed above: Because she was intoxicated (under the influence of alcohol), she was unable to consent to having sex with Jason.

Unfortunately, such incidents are becoming increasingly common. In the past several years, a drug called Rohypnol, which is illegal in the United States and known on the street as roofies or roapies, has gained a reputation as the "date rape drug." Females from all over the United States have reported being raped after an attacker slipped the drug into their drinks without their knowledge. Because Rohypnol has no smell or taste, victims are unable to detect it. After only a few minutes, Rohypnol causes the victim to feel dizzy, confused, and nauseated. She may have trouble speaking and moving, and may pass out. A victim will usually have no memory of what happened to her while under the influence of the drug.

Who Are the Victims?

Victims of rape can be young or old, rich or poor. Rape can happen at work or school, on the street, or in your own home. According to a 1999 survey conducted by the American College of Obstetrics and Gynecology:

Rapists are often known to their victims as acquaintances or friends.

- Over half of first-time rape victims are under eighteen. Almost a quarter are under twelve.

- More than 75 percent of adolescent rape victims are raped by an acquaintance, such as a relative, a family friend, a schoolmate, or a date.

- Over 80 percent of sexual assaults involve a weapon or the threat of physical harm.

Who Are the Rapists?

Many people imagine the typical rapist to be a stranger waiting in a dark alley or behind the bushes for a vulnerable-looking woman to walk by. This kind of rapist certainly exists, but as you can see from the statistics listed, the vast majority of adolescent rape victims are raped by an acquaintance. This is true in the general population as well—the majority of all rapes are committed by someone known to the victim. These "acquaintance" rapists usually do not look different or act differently than anyone else.

Acquaintance or Date Rape

Rapists who are known to their victims can be acquaintances, friends, relatives, neighbors, or other familiar people. The rapist can be a husband, a steady boyfriend, or a casual friend who forces the victim to have sex.

These men may be shocked to be called rapists. They don't consider their actions to be rape. Because of cultural stereotypes about men and women's roles in society, they may assume that they have the right to do what they did. And they often rape again, either the same person or someone else, because of these misconceptions.

Stranger and Serial Rapists

Many people don't know how common acquaintance rape is because it is rarely reported in the media. The kind of rape that we do hear about in the news tends to involve rapists who attack strangers or select victims at random. These assailants plan their attacks and may rape more than one woman in a neighborhood. Men who rape multiple victims in a specific area or over a given period of time are known as serial rapists and can hold whole communities in fear.

Chapter Two

Some Misunderstandings About Rape

I've never been raped, but a few weeks ago I was drunk in my boyfriend Eric's dorm room, and he pushed me down on the bed and tried to take my clothes off. Even though I was pretty drunk, I knew I didn't want to have sex. What really surprised me was that his buddy, who was also a friend of mine, tried to tell me that I owed it to Eric because I'd gotten drunk on their beer! I was really glad I hadn't passed out or anything because I think he would have had sex with me while I was unconscious.

Everyone has different ideas about the proper roles of men and women in society, and it can be difficult to figure out where you stand on certain issues. Teenagers in particular can be confused about gender roles, since part of being a teen means figuring out how adult females and males behave. A male teen may think that he has to act super-macho and "score" often so that other guys won't call him a loser. A female teen may feel that she has to go along with whatever a guy wants in order to be popular or to keep him interested in dating her.

In a recent study, male and female teens age fourteen to eighteen were asked to judge the following statements as true or false:

- If a girl kisses a guy and he gets turned on, he has the right to have sex with her.

- If a girl goes somewhere alone with a guy, it means she intends to have sex with him.

- If a guy spends a lot of money on a date, she owes him sex.

- If a girl dresses in a sexy outfit, she is asking for sex.

- If a girl has had sex with a guy before, he can have sex with her again any time he wants.

- If she didn't scream, it wasn't rape.

- A good-looking or popular guy is never a rapist because he can get all the sex he wants.

The correct answer to all of those statements is

Young men often feel pressure to act macho in front of friends.

FALSE. A man never has the right to force sex upon a woman, no matter what their relationship. A person—woman or man—always has the right to control what happens to her or his own body and to say no to sex at any time.

But the results of the study show that many teens are unaware of their rights and unclear about how rape is defined. Almost two-thirds of the males and almost half of the females who responded to the survey answered "true" to *all* of the questions.

When a girl believes these kinds of messages, it puts her at a disadvantage. She is more likely to be coerced into having sex, and she is less likely to report or tell anyone about having been raped. She may feel guilty because she thinks that she "asked for it" and brought the attack on herself. She is also less likely to believe and support another female who has been raped.

Guys who believe these messages also need to take a good look at themselves. These beliefs put them at risk of becoming rapists by not listening to a date when she says no to sex. In addition, these guys may find themselves feeling guilty for having sex with a girl just to be able to say that they "scored" when they actually didn't want to have sex at all. Male victims of rape who believe that the survey statements are true also risk feeling the additional guilt and shame of thinking that they failed to live up to society's standards of real manhood.

Who Gets Raped?

Another common misconception about rape is that only young, attractive women get raped. In fact, rape can happen to anyone at any age. Sexual abuse, including intercourse, can happen to infants and toddlers as well as older women and men. Eighty-year-old women have been raped in their own homes during burglaries.

Rape is about power, not sexual attraction. Today rape is even being used as a weapon of war by armies in Kosovo, part of the former Yugoslavia. Rape is used to weaken the enemy mentally by violating defenseless women and making the men of the society ashamed

Many teens are confused about what is and what is not rape.

that they are unable to protect their wives, daughters, grandmothers, cousins, and friends.

Where Do These Misunderstandings Come From?

It is no wonder that teens have misunderstandings about the meaning of rape. These kinds of misconceptions are being spread every day throughout the world. For example, women all over Italy are currently in an uproar over a 1999 decision by the Italian government that sex—even unwanted sex—with a woman wearing jeans can never be considered rape. How does Italy's equivalent of the Supreme Court explain the reasoning behind its decision? Because jeans are so difficult to remove, the court claims, the woman must have helped the man remove her clothing, and so she couldn't have been protesting the sexual act.

In 1990, a female jogger was beaten and raped in New York City's Central Park. Instead of feeling pity for the victim and anger at the attackers, many people first reacted by saying, "Well, what was she doing there alone anyway?"—as if the crime were the victim's fault. No matter what time of day or night rape happens, no matter where it occurs or to whom it happens, rape is never the victim's fault.

Chapter Three

Prevention

I'll never really know if it was my imagination or what, but I think someone was stalking me on my way home from school. Whenever I looked around, this guy was behind me, even when I turned a corner or crossed the street. He started off almost a block behind me and was getting closer, maybe a hundred feet. So I ducked into a store and called my mom to come and get me.

The best way to protect yourself from sexual assault is to be aware of yourself and your surroundings and to prepare yourself for any kind of attack. Think about the possibility of rape and what you would do in that situation. Would you fight back and scream for help? Would you try talking or joking your attacker out of it?

Trust your instincts if you believe that you are being followed, and get to a safe place fast.

Imagine ways that an attack could happen and practice possible responses to them. Practice will help you to keep your cool and act quickly should you ever find yourself in a real-life emergency.

Outside the Home

Many rapes happen outside the home during the course of normal daily activities. There are steps you can take to protect yourself, however. Walking in a hesitant and unsure way signals fear and timidity—in other words, it makes you look like an easy victim. When walking alone or in areas that you don't know well, stand up straight and walk confidently, with your head up. Even if you don't know the way, always look like you know where you are and where you are going. If you need to look at a map or ask for directions, go into a store or a building lobby.

Trust your instincts. Does it seem as if someone is following you? If something doesn't feel right, immediately go to a well-lit area with lots of people. Walk in the middle of the sidewalk whenever possible. Don't get too close to doorways, bushes, or alleys where an attacker could hide. Keep away from cars, too. If someone stops and asks you for directions, answer from a distance and walk away if the person gets out of the car and starts walking toward you. Finally, walk with friends whenever possible. There *is* safety in numbers.

Do not open the door under any circumstances when you are home alone.

At Home

Never open your door without knowing who is outside. Always ask to see the identification of a repairperson before opening the door for him or her. If you are not expecting anyone, ask for the person's office number and call before letting him or her inside to make sure that this person is actually supposed to be there.

If strangers ask to use your telephone to make an emergency call, offer to take the number and make the call yourself. Have them wait outside while you call. Never admit that you are home alone to a stranger at the door or a caller on the phone. If you come home and find an open door or a broken window, do not go inside. Go to the nearest phone and call 911 or the police.

On a Date

Let's say that you decide that you are not ready for a sexual relationship with a guy. How can you communicate that to him? One way is to stay away from situations where you might experience pressure to have sex. Go on group dates with friends rather than pairing off. Don't drink alcohol or do drugs. Some people use drugs or alcohol to feel more comfortable in a new social situation, but as you lose your shyness you may also lose the wariness and clear thinking that could warn you of a dangerous situation. If you do drink and you feel drowsy or faint, get help as soon as you can. Someone may have given you Rohypnol or another similar drug to make you pass out.

If you are kissing and touching with someone you aren't ready to have sex with and you want to stop, make sure that your "no" is very clear. Many guys mistakenly believe that girls really want to have sex even when they say no. Even the nicest guy will sometimes keep going after you ask him to stop. If that happens, say no again. If that does not work, say it again—louder. Move away from him. Turn on the lights. Start a conversation. If he still doesn't stop, scream or shout for help. Don't be afraid of hurting his feelings or causing a scene. Being forced to have sex is much worse than making a scene.

Chapter Four

What to Do If You Are Attacked

I joke about everything. That's how I deal with difficult situations. Instead of getting upset, I tell a joke and make myself and anyone else around me laugh. So when this guy grabbed me in the alley with a chokehold around my neck, my first reaction was to start talking. I actually made him laugh. He loosened his hold and I ran to the nearest store. I am convinced that the only reason I escaped was that I distracted my attacker and caught him off guard.

There is no advice that can absolutely guarantee that you will never be a victim of sexual assault. There are some things that may be helpful to know, however.

If you have prepared for dangerous situations by thinking ahead of time about ways to protect yourself, you will have more options to choose from if the event actually occurs. Think about whether you would be able to fight back if it meant hitting hard enough to seriously hurt your attacker.

Remember that rape is a violent crime and that the rapist most probably is willing to use force. If you are attacked, your first thought must always be your own safety. If you can stay cool and calm, you will be better able to think fast in order to get away. Whatever happens, if you survive, you did the right thing.

Passive Resistance

Some people, like the girl in the beginning of this chapter, are more comfortable than others trying to talk their way out of a dangerous situation. This is called passive resistance. Some examples of this are:

- Talking to the assailant and trying to persuade him not to attack. If you distract him, you may be able to escape.

- Telling him that you have AIDS or another sexually transmitted disease, like herpes, that he could acquire from having sex with you. Even if he still rapes you, he may be willing to use a condom.

- Crying hysterically, acting crazy, vomiting, or pretending to faint.

- ◆ If you are at or near home, telling him that your parents or your brother will be coming home any minute.

Active Resistance

Here are some ways to actively resist:

- ◆ Screaming can surprise the attacker or scare him away if he thinks that someone may hear and come to help you.

- ◆ Fighting back may also surprise him and make him stop or give you an opportunity to escape. But you have to hit or kick hard enough to really hurt your attacker. Aim at tender spots like the groin, eyes, or shins. The downside of this response is that it can escalate (raise) the level of violence that he is willing to use against you.

- ◆ Some people carry weapons, such as a gun, knife, or pepper spray. This can be a bad idea, however, because if you hesitate for even a split second, it is extremely easy for the attacker to grab your weapon and use it against you.

To be prepared, the best thing you can do is to get trained in self-defense. Some organizations, including

Self-defense techniques enable you to fight back effectively.

universities, YMCAs, and community centers, host special self-defense clinics to teach women how to stay aware and how to fight back without putting themselves in more danger. You can also learn self-defense techniques such as karate, aikido, and other martial arts. Check your neighborhood community centers for martial arts classes, or contact one of the organizations listed in the back of this book.

Chapter Five

If You Have Been Raped

*A*fter he left I felt so dirty, like my whole body was covered in slime. All I wanted was to be clean again. I stood in the shower for over an hour, even after all the hot water had run out, and scrubbed myself with soap over and over again.

The First Few Hours

After a sexual assault, the victim often feels dirty, and her first urge is to scrub herself clean. Do not do that! Even if you have not decided whether to press charges or be a witness, it is extremely important to get a medical exam immediately. You can always decide later not to use the evidence. Once you have showered and washed your clothes, however, much of the evidence is gone for good.

If you have been raped, do not wash, douche, change

clothes, or destroy valuable evidence in any other way. Even a strand of hair can be important evidence. It is best if evidence is collected within twelve hours of the attack, but it can be collected up to seventy-two hours afterward. For the same reasons, do not clean up your house if the attack occurred there.

It is vital to report a rape to the police. Statistics show that most rapists repeat their crimes. If your report helps lead to the capture of a rapist, you will have protected countless other potential victims. Many women also find that reporting their rape gives them a sense of control over the situation. Although they were helpless during the attack, they still have the ability to make important choices about events that happen to them.

Getting Help

If you have been the victim of rape, the first thing to do in all cases is to get help—fast. There are many places to go for help. You may be scared or in shock about what has happened, and it can be hard to think straight. Call someone who can protect you and help you through the first few hours.

If you have any fear that the rapist may come back and hurt you again, go somewhere that you feel safe—preferably a friend or relative's house. If you have been injured, the police will take you to an emergency room for medical care.

When you call the police emergency number to

It is vital that victims report rape and sexual assault to the police.

report that you have been raped, you can expect to be asked for the following information by the police or emergency dispatcher over the telephone:

- Your name and location

- How long ago the assault occurred

- A brief description of the rapist, if he had a vehicle, and the direction he was last seen heading

- If the rapist had a weapon

Many communities now have a special sexual assault team made up of officers who have received special training in dealing with rape victims. They understand how frightening rape can be and how difficult it is for many women to talk about the event or to press charges.

You can find phone numbers for rape crisis hotlines in the yellow pages of the phone book under Crisis Intervention Services, Social Service Organizations, or Women's Organizations. A crisis counselor can help you to make decisions about what to do. Some organizations even have counselors who will come with the police to act as your protector during any investigation. They can also provide ongoing counseling and support in the weeks after the assault while you heal.

Although you may want to tell a trusted friend or family member what has happened, you may have trouble choosing a relative or friend to talk to. If the rapist was a friend or acquaintance, you might feel like you can no longer tell who is trustworthy.

The Next Steps

Once you have chosen someone to help you make decisions, go immediately to a hospital emergency room or clinic. It is important to ensure that you have not been injured, impregnated, or exposed to a sexually transmitted disease. If you are not taking some kind of ongoing birth control like the pill or Depo Provera, you will need to decide whether to get emergency contraception, also called the morning-after pill. Emergency contraception can prevent you from getting pregnant up to seventy-two hours after intercourse occurs. The morning-after pill is actually a very high dose of a regular birth control pill. Between two and eight pills

After an attack, it is important to see a doctor, no matter how upset or traumatized you feel.

are taken within seventy-two hours of intercourse, followed by a second dose twelve hours later. Not all birth control pills work as morning-after pills, and the number of pills needed varies depending on the brand, so it is important to talk to a doctor or nurse to make sure you are getting the right kind in the correct dosage.

The doctor or nurse practitioner can give you antibiotics to prevent the onset (beginning) of a sexually transmitted infection. Antibiotics can treat only bacterial infections like gonorrhea or chlamydia, however. Ask about protection from viral infections like hepatitis or HIV. Preventive treatment for these diseases is more complicated and may require a series of shots or taking pills several times a day for a month or more. You may also need to go back to the doctor in six weeks for follow-up testing to be sure that no new problems have developed.

The Evidenciary Exam

At the hospital or clinic, you will have an opportunity to undergo an evidenciary exam. This is best done as soon as possible after the rape. It involves a careful examination of the victim's clothing and body and gathering any traces the assailant may have left behind, such as semen, hair, or threads from his clothing. The examiner may take photographs of injuries for evidence. This helps the police to support the information you have given them about the attack.

The examiner will probably perform a speculum exam of your vagina. This involves putting a warmed instrument shaped like a duck's bill into the vagina to open it, so the examiner can check for internal damage or take samples for testing. It doesn't usually hurt, but it may if there are vaginal injuries. Usually it just feels strange.

The thought of having more strangers look at your body after you have been assaulted and invaded by a rapist can be very unpleasant. Even if you decide not to press charges, however, it is very important to be checked for injuries and to receive protection against pregnancy and disease. Some women feel more comfortable when the examiner is a woman. You can request that a female physician or nurse practitioner perform the exam.

Chapter Six

To Report or Not to Report?

My husband and I were in the middle of a divorce. I had a court order telling him to stay away from me except when picking up or dropping off the kids. He had been abusive for a long time, but I was ready to stand up for myself and not take it anymore. I had my own job, I was healthy, and friends thought I was doing a good job being a single mom.

One night I woke up to find my husband standing over me with the television in his hands, ready to smash my head with it. He threw it onto the floor instead, then jumped on me and raped me.

As soon as he left, I called the police. I was ashamed that I had let him frighten me and hadn't fought him off, but the nurse examiner *told me that I had done the right thing. I had survived the attack, which might not have been the case if I'd fought back physically, and I was fighting back now by reporting him. I hadn't thought about it that way, and it made me feel a lot better.*

Sometimes it can be hard to decide whether to report a rape to the police. You may feel that no one will believe you, especially if your attacker was an acquaintance. Maybe you are afraid that you will be blamed for what happened. Or perhaps the thought of having an exam and telling the story is too upsetting. In some cases of acquaintance rape, the victim may feel violated but may not realize at first that she has been sexually assaulted. It may take a day or two for that to sink in.

Things to Think About

All of those feelings are real and important to consider, but it is still essential to think seriously about reporting the attack. For one thing, most rapists repeat the crime again and again. If he is not caught, he may attack another woman in the neighborhood. Also, many women feel that they regain some control over their lives by reporting. Reporting the attack is like saying to the rapist: "My body is mine and my feelings and life are valuable. You can't do this to me or to anybody else.

What you did was wrong!" Instead of continuing to be a victim, you are making yourself the one in charge.

As attitudes about rape change, more and more communities are developing special teams of counselors and trained police officers who work together on sexual assault cases. These team members work with the district attorney's office in prosecuting offenders and are specially trained to be sensitive to the victim's feelings and to ensure that the investigation does not add to her trauma.

Court rulings have made it more difficult for a defense attorney (the lawyer defending the rape suspect) to make the victim seem like a bad person by exposing any past sexual experiences she may have had. If there is evidence from a professional exam performed soon after the attack, many cases don't even go to trial; the rapist often pleads guilty, hoping to get a lighter sentence. Women's groups provide support during the investigation as well as the trial and offer individual and group counseling to help the victim heal.

Chapter Seven

If Your Friend Is the Victim

*W*hen Maura told me that Tom had raped her, my first thought was, "That's not possible— Tom's a good guy." But I'm glad I just listened and didn't say anything. Maura said later that just having me listen to her and believe her made it okay for her to take the next step and go talk to a counselor about it.

How Can I Help?

If your friend is the victim of rape, she needs you to be there to listen to her. Sometimes the most important thing for a person to do is to talk about anything and everything—what happened, what she did, what he did, what she should have done, what he could have

If your friend has been raped, being a good listener is the best way to help.

done. Your friend may need to tell her story long after you think she "should" be over it. But the best thing you can do is listen, as many times as she needs to talk about it, and tell her how glad you are that she survived. Don't be afraid to listen and not say anything. It is the listening that is important.

If you think that your friend did something wrong or silly that got her into trouble, do not say so—at least not now. Right after the attack, she needs unconditional support and love, not "You should have done this" or "You shouldn't have done that." Those things are easy for you to say, looking back at what happened. But being raped was not her fault, no matter what she did, and you need to keep telling her that.

Many times we want to place the blame on the victim

because it makes us feel safer: We wouldn't be so dumb as to do what she did; we could never be raped. But our feelings aren't important at this time—the victim's feelings are. It is essential to tell her what will help her heal, not what will make us feel better.

Keep what your friend tells you to yourself. She probably is already feeling violated and does not need to be further violated by having to face everyone in school, knowing that they know all the details. If she wants anyone besides you to know, she will tell them herself.

It is easy to get angry for your friend and to want to take care of her. She has had control of her body taken away from her. Part of her healing will be regaining a feeling of control over her life by making her own decisions. You can encourage her to report the attack or recommend that she get counseling, and you can even look up phone numbers for her. But it is up to her to make the decision and to make the calls. You can be there for her, but let her do things for herself. Healing can occur as part of simple day-to-day events like getting up in the morning, choosing what clothes to wear, and walking down the street with friends.

If your friend won't make contact with the police or talk to a counselor, consider calling and getting information for yourself. The rape crisis center may have some suggestions for ways you can help your friend until she is ready to get help for herself. It is also important for you to be able to talk to someone in order to deal with your own feelings, worries, and fears.

What to Expect

Healing takes time, and friends sometimes burn out. They think, "It has been six weeks [or six months, or a year] and she's still talking about it and acting strange. Why doesn't she just get over it?" It can be a long time before your friend recovers completely. She will probably need to talk about the rape less as time goes on, but the subject may come up months or years later. Be patient and let her move through the recovery process at her own speed.

Your friend may act like somebody else for a while—even someone you don't know and may not like. The damage to her sense of personal safety and to her sense of identity may cause her to do things that are completely out of character. The following are some possible examples:

- She may stay away from certain activities or from people, or may start acting like a small child.

- She may feel as if nothing matters anymore and start breaking rules at school, running away from home, or sleeping around. She may go from an A or B student to a D or F student.

- She may suddenly start to use drugs or alcohol

to numb her painful feelings.

- She may punish herself with self-mutilation (burning herself with a lighter, cutting herself) or by starving herself or throwing up whatever she eats. Or she may gain huge amounts of weight in a short period of time in an effort to make herself ugly to men and thus, in her mind, less likely to be raped.

Stick with It

If you notice these behaviors in your friend, let her know that you see that she is acting differently than usual, and ask her why. She may tell you what is happening inside, or she may not. Either way, don't stop being her friend. Behavior changes this dramatic mean that something is wrong, so don't turn away from her. Consider talking to a school counselor or another trusted adult. If you see these behaviors when you already know she's a rape victim, encourage her to get counseling or to call a rape crisis line for help.

Victims often turn to drugs and alcohol to numb their feelings.

Chapter Eight

Healing

A friend of my brother's, a guy I thought was also a friend of mine, asked me to get pizza with him after a party. On the way, he drove the car onto a side street, locked the door, wedged my head between the armrest and the seat, and raped me.

I tried to push him away and started to cry, but he was bigger and stronger and I couldn't move with him on top of me. I still get panicky if I start to feel trapped under my boyfriend, even though we have been going out for three years and I know he loves me and wouldn't do anything to hurt me. I've told him about it and he is very careful with me, but I'm not sure any guy can understand what it feels like to be trapped like that.

Post-Traumatic Stress Disorder

Stage One: Acute Anxiety

Each person recovers from a violent crime like rape at his or her own speed and in his or her own way. In general, however, recovery is a long process. It does not happen overnight. Post-traumatic stress disorder (PTSD) describes the recovery process that many victims of a traumatic event go through, whether the event is a natural disaster like an earthquake or a tornado, a war, or a rape.

For most victims, the first stage of PTSD is a phase of extreme anxiety, fear, or stress and can last anywhere from a few days to six months or more. Stress is a normal response to change and can be protective when it causes you to be more alert to possible signs of danger. When the fear and anxiety are so intense that you can't pay attention to anything else, however, it becomes harmful.

Panic Attacks

Victims may suffer from panic attacks, in which they feel intense fear and think that they are about to die, or from episodes of hyperventilation, in which they feel as if they can't breathe. Victims also may be afraid to be alone. They may obsessively check door and window locks, inside closets, or under beds because no place feels safe anymore. They may jump

Anxiety may cause survivors to obsessively check locks on doors and windows.

at a loud noise or if someone touches them unexpect-edly. Flashbacks may occur without warning, during which the victim is forced to relive the event over and over again in his or her head.

Guilt and Shame

Feelings of excessive guilt also are common. Trying to make some sense out of a senseless act, the victim blames him- or herself for allowing the attack to happen. There is also a sense of shame for having been so helpless.

Denial

Sometimes the feelings associated with rape are so painful that victims either will deny that anything

Relaxation techniques such as meditation can help victims to heal.

happened or will become numb and disconnected, seeing the event from the viewpoint of a spectator as if it had happened to someone else. They may withdraw from all human contact. They may drink or take drugs to try to forget or to medicate a panic attack.

Healthy Healing: Relaxation Techniques

One healthy way to respond to these feelings is to use conscious relaxation techniques. Find a picture of a happy event in your life. Prop it up so you can see it easily from a relaxed position in a comfortable chair. Dim the lights. Concentrate on your breathing, making it slow, deep, and relaxed. Feel your body becoming relaxed. Feel the tension leaving your face, neck, back, and legs.

Keeping your attention focused on the picture, try to bring back the feelings of contentment you had at the time the picture was taken. If scary feelings try to slip in, gently push them away and bring your attention back to the picture. Continue to breathe slowly and deeply. When you are ready to stop, take a few more deep breaths and stretch your whole body before standing up. This technique can be helpful whenever you are feeling stressed out.

Stage Two: Reorganization

The second phase of PTSD is called reorganization. The victim looks normal on the outside and seems to be functioning adequately in daily tasks. Because he or she appears to be okay, friends may not pay as close attention or not be as supportive as before, especially if the victim starts acting out in ways that are different or unacceptable. Some common ways that victims act out are running away from home, quitting school, acting wild and angry all the time, and pulling away from old friends.

The truth is, on the inside, your friend is still feeling anger, guilt, shame, fear, and depression. Victims may feel numb and disconnected from themselves and from other people. They may not feel that they can trust anyone.

At this stage, one-to-one counseling may be helpful. Survivors groups, where victims can share their feelings and hear how others are feeling and coping with rape trauma, can also be helpful at this time. In the acute phase, listening to others' experiences can be too frightening. During reorganization, however, it can be comforting to know that there are other people who are having similar feelings and that the victim is not alone.

The Final Stage:
From Victim to Survivor

During the final stage, the person changes from victim to survivor. A victim is someone whom events happen to and whose responses are controlled by the past. A survivor may still have painful feelings and memories but makes choices and decisions based on his or her needs today and his or her plans for tomorrow. A survivor decides every day not to let the past control the future.

The survivor becomes more involved in his or her life and begins to experience joy again. He or she is able to turn more attention outward, away from him- or herself, and to see other people's needs. By actively choosing how they are going to feel or react in response to life events, survivors regain a sense of control and are able to reconnect with other people and build relationships.

Some of the ways survivors can take control are to join a book group, take a class in a subject they've

Survivors benefit from challenging themselves with new experiences.

always wanted to know more about, or join a sports team. Some take self-defense classes like karate or kickboxing. Others continue to participate in group therapy, but instead of focusing on their own fears, they may find themselves a leader in the group, helping others to find their way. Survivors challenge themselves with new activities and experiences.

These stages of recovery are not always easily identified, and people commonly move back and forth between stages several times before being able to move on completely. For example, even someone in the last stage of recovery may still have a bad experience that brings back frightening memories and causes the person to temporarily slip back into numbness or

withdrawal. Without help, many people find it difficult to move beyond depression into survival.
Counseling, antidepressant medications, or both may
be needed to help someone move out of depression
and toward confidence.

Healing takes time, effort, and the support of family
and friends. Many people who have survived rape
trauma find that they emerge from the experience
stronger, wiser, and more compassionate toward others.

Chapter Nine

Victims' Rights

If you or someone you know has been raped, it is vital to know about victims' rights, the resources available to victims, and what victims can—and should—expect from the police, doctors and nurses, and the law.

Your Personal Rights

- Feel free to ask questions of police, doctors, attorneys, counselors, or agency employees.

- Remember, no matter how it came about, the rape was not your fault.

- It is normal to feel guilty, fearful, lonely, or helpless.

- It is normal to feel emotionless, numb, and hysterical. These are all symptoms of rape trauma syndrome.

- It is normal, and often healthy, to cry.

- It is all right to want to be treated like a special person.

- You have the right to be loved—you have done nothing wrong.

Your Legal Rights

You have the right to:

- Report the assault to law enforcement and to expect that all avenues within the law will be pursued to apprehend and convict the offender.

- File a third party report (for example, a rape crisis center reports the crime but does not disclose your name).

- Do nothing. However, many women who report their rape feel stronger and recover more effectively by taking positive action to aid law enforcement officers in capturing and prosecuting their rapist. Remember, most rapists will repeat their crime. By reporting the crime, you may prevent another attack on you or on someone else.

- Be treated in a considerate, sensitive manner by law enforcement and prosecution personnel during the investigation and trial.

- Ask if a female officer is available to conduct the initial investigation.

- Change or add to your initial statement as you start to recall details clearly. Be sure to obtain the investigating officer's name and telephone number in case you remember important details about the rape at a later time.

Your Medical Rights

You have the right to:

- Have a rape crisis counselor accompany you to the hospital

- Privacy, gentleness, and sensitivity during the interview and examination

- Have an explanation of the reason for every test, form, and procedure

- Have all medical testing necessary for evidence collection paid for by the law enforcement agency in whose jurisdiction the crime occurred

- Follow-up treatment, tests, and counseling

(Adapted from the *Sexual Assault Prevention Handbook,* published by the Crime and Violence Prevention Center of the Office of the Attorney General of the State of California.)

Glossary

acquaintance rape Forced sexual intercourse or other sexual acts between acquaintances (people who know each other).

active resistance Getting out of a dangerous situation by fighting back.

assault Attempt or threat to cause injury to another person.

date rape Forced sexual intercourse or other sexual acts between people who are dating.

evidence Facts or proof that an event happened.

evidenciary exam Physical and/or mental exam of a victim performed as soon as possible after an incident to search for evidence.

morning-after pill (emergency contraception) Pills taken within seventy-two hours after intercourse in order to prevent pregnancy.

passive resistance Escaping from a dangerous situation without using force.

psychiatrist Licensed medical doctor who is trained to diagnose, treat, and prevent mental illness.

psychologist Someone who studies the science of mind and behavior.

rape (sexual assault) Any form of sexual behavior carried out upon someone against his or her will.

Rohypnol Sometimes called the "date rape drug," this illegal substance causes memory loss and is used by some rapists on their victims.

serial rapists Rapists who rape multiple victims in an area or community or over a given period of time.

sexually transmitted disease (STD) A disease, such as gonorrhea, chlamydia, and HIV, that is spread through sexual activity.

speculum exam Exam of the vagina using a speculum (a special instrument for opening the vagina) to search for internal damage or take samples for testing.

stalking Following someone in a furtive (sneaky) or persistent way.

trauma An event that causes physical harm and/or serious emotional stress.

trial Examination in front of a judge and/or jury of facts and law concerning an event.

Where to Go for Help

You can look in your local yellow pages under Crisis Intervention Services, Social Service Organizations, and Women's Organizations and Services to find agencies listed in your area, or you can try the following:

In the United States

Emergency Contraception Hotline
(800) NOT-2-LATE

Planned Parenthood Federation of America
810 Seventh Avenue
New York, NY 10019
(800) 230-7526
Web site: http://www.ppfa.org/ppfa

PrePare Self-Defense
145 West 25th Street
New York, NY 10001
(800) 442-7273

The Rape, Abuse, and Incest National
        Network (RAINN)
252 10th St. NE
Washington, DC 20002
(800) 656-4673
Web site: http://www.rainn.org

In Canada

Ontario Coalition Rape Crisis Centre
(705) 268-8381

Planned Parenthood Federation of Canada
1 Nicholas Street, Suite 430
Ottowa, ON K1Z 8R1
(613) 238-4474
Web site: http://www.ppfc.org

Toronto Rape Crisis Centre Hotline
(416) 597-8808

For Further Reading

Bandon, Alexandra. *Date Rape.* Columbus, OH: Silver Burdett Press, 1994.

Jukes, Mavis. *It's a Girl Thing: How to Stay Healthy, Safe, and in Charge.* New York: Alfred A. Knopf, 1996.

Kaminker, Laura. *Everything You Need to Know About Dealing with Sexual Assault.* New York: Rosen Publishing Group, 1998.

La Valle, John. *Everything You Need to Know When You Are the Male Survivor of Rape or Sexual Assault.* New York: Rosen Publishing Group, 1996.

Parrot, Andrea. *Coping with Date Rape and Acquaintance Rape.* New York: Rosen Publishing Group, 1995.

Stoppard, Miriam. *Sex Ed: Growing Up, Relationships, and Sex.* New York: DK Publishing, 1998.

Zvirin, Stephanie. *The Best Years of Their Lives: A Resource Guide for Teens in Crisis.* Chicago: American Library Association, 1992.

Women's Rights Handbook
Contains valuable information on rape, legal proceedings, and women's legal rights. To order a free copy, write to:

Public Inquiry Unit
Office of the Attorney General
P.O. Box 944255
Sacramento, CA 94244-2550

Index

About the Author

Cheryl Branch Coppin is a family nurse practitioner living in northern California and has specialized in women's health care for over twenty years. Currently, she is a nurse examiner for sexual assault victims, for the screening of breast and cervical cancer, and for the screening and treatment of sexually transmitted infection. Coppin is also a clinician in public family-planning clinics. She has two beautiful daughters who are grown up, and two yellow labs who will never grow up.

Photo Credits

Cover and interior shots by Ira Fox except p.30 by John Betham.

Design and Layout

Laura Murawski